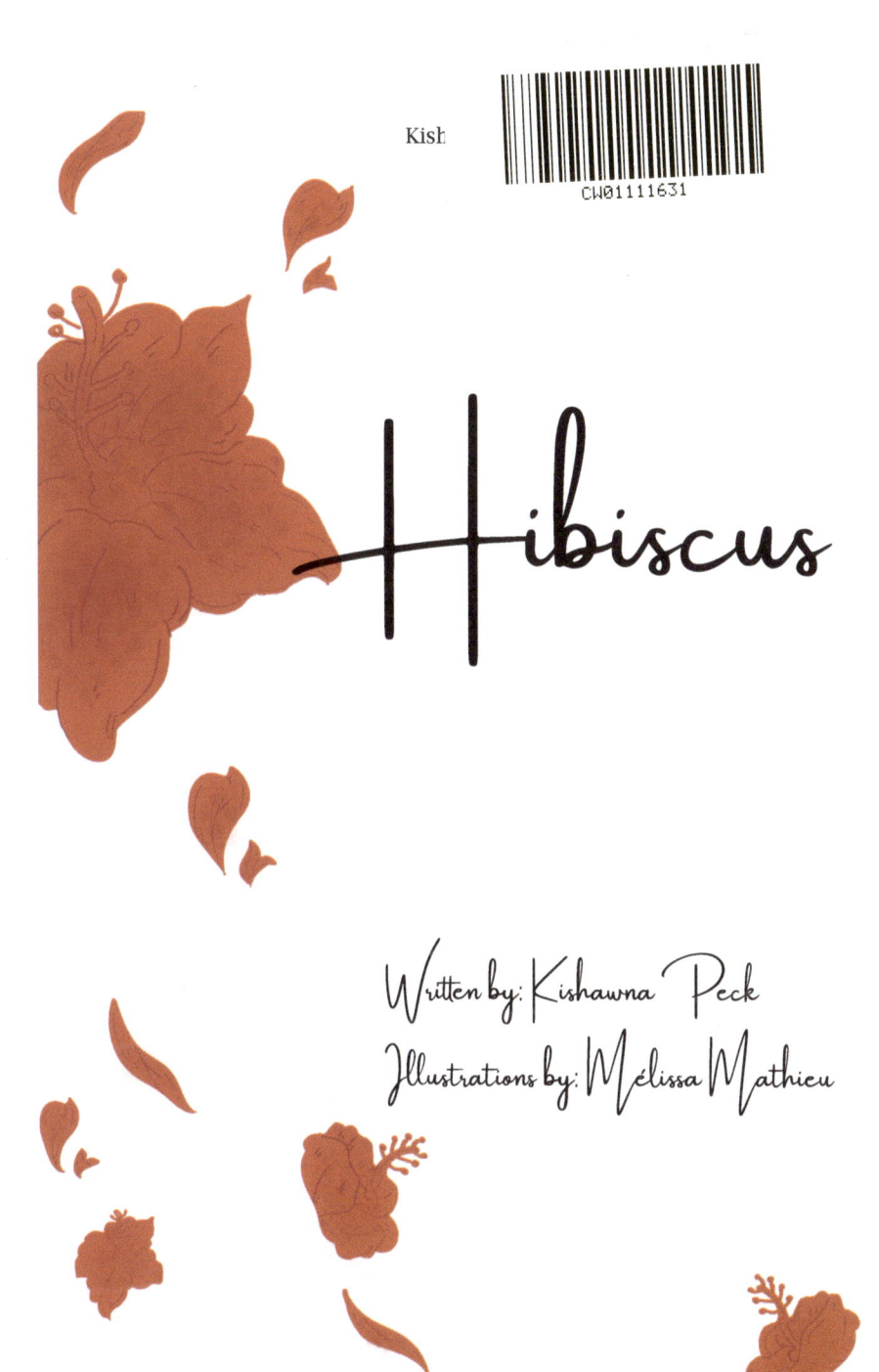

Hibiscus

Written by: Kishawna Peck

Illustrations by: Mélissa Mathieu

Hibiscus

Author: Kishawna Peck
Illustrator: Mélissa Mathieu
Copyright © 2020 Kishawna Peck. All rights reserved.
Published by I Am Kishawna
ISBN 978-1-7775019-0-7

All rights reserved. No part of this book may be reproduced or used in any manner without written permission of the copyright owner except for the use of quotations in a book review.
For more information email: iamkishawna@gmail.com
All adaptations of the Work for film, theatre, television and radio are strictly prohibited.

I Am Kishawna books may be purchased for educational, business or sales promotional use.

For more information, please email the Sales Department at iamkishawna@gmail.com

www.kishawna.com

Kishawna

Dedicated to all the womxn who taught me how to love and to continue to be my unapologetic self.

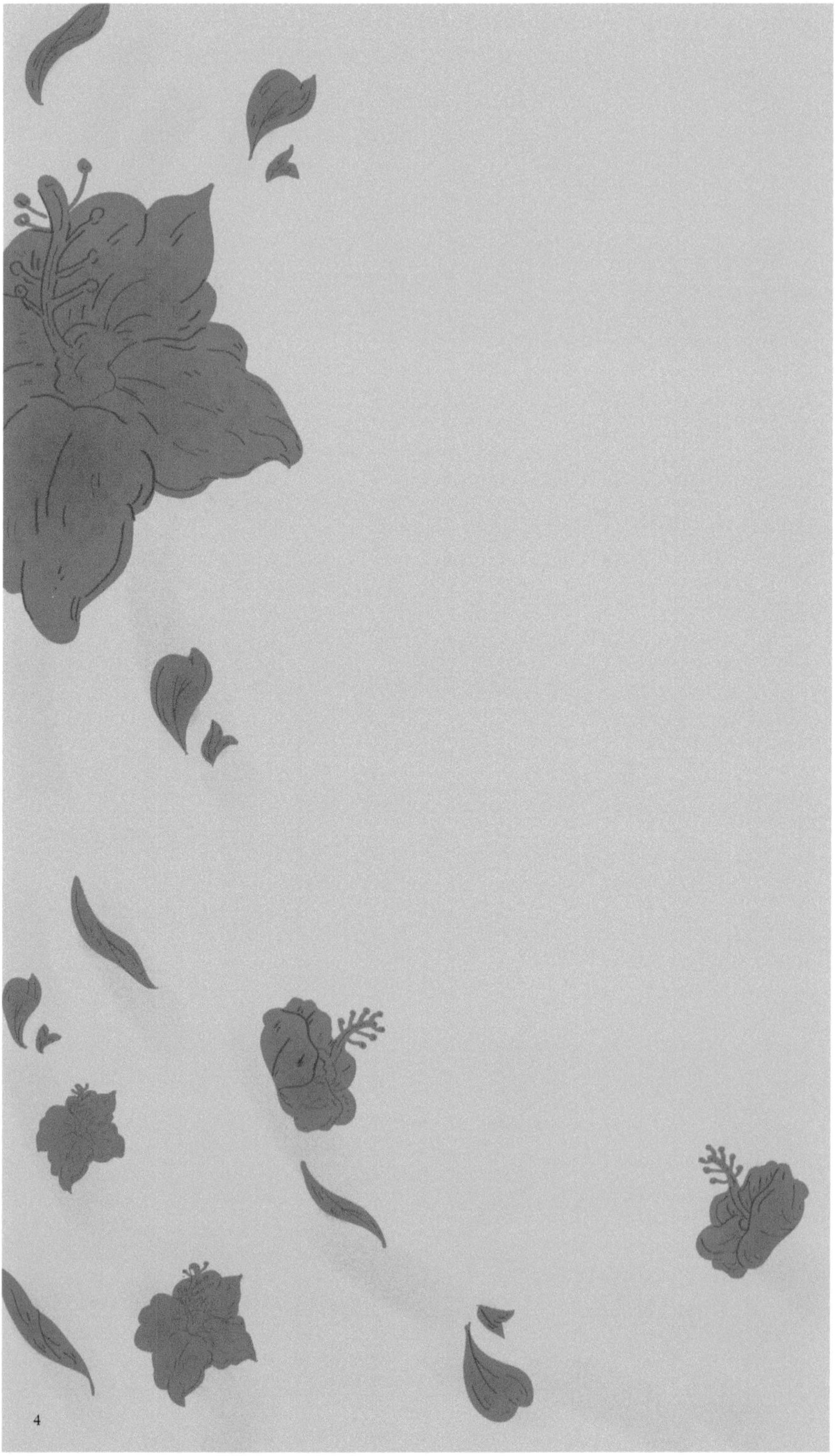

Contents

Love & Lust	11
Mental Wellness & Self Care	43
Work & Career	59
Sorrel Recipe	76

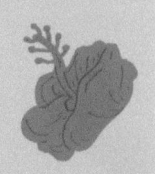

Hibiscus

Foreword

With every keystroke and stroke of my pen, I'm slowly undressing in broad daylight on a crowded street. Yes. It's that serious!

In celebration of my unravelling, I've left a seat up front just for you. Don't be shy, get comfortable, grab a glass of wine or two, and let's do this!

P.S There's a special sorrel recipe on page 76 for your indulgence. Sorrel is a traditional Jamaican drink made with dried hibiscus leaves and packed with festive flavours. It reminds me of family gatherings, laughter, and my roots.

With love,
Kishawna

Mama

Nutmeg
Cinnamon
and a pinch of allspice
Stew peas
Plantain
and a side of white rice

How the music sweet you
know you hail from paradise
"Dance how you feel"
one of my favourite advice

Warmer embraces never coulda exist
Mini skirts
Wickedest skank
Forever my empress

Feel you with me
when I wash dishes by the sink
Or when I'm doubtful
whispering
"Enjoy yourself it's later than you think"

You would have wanted me
to live like it's my last
Let myself go
Shed the costumes and the masks
Laugh and love
and discover my life's task

Mama
Journal's out and sorrel in my glass

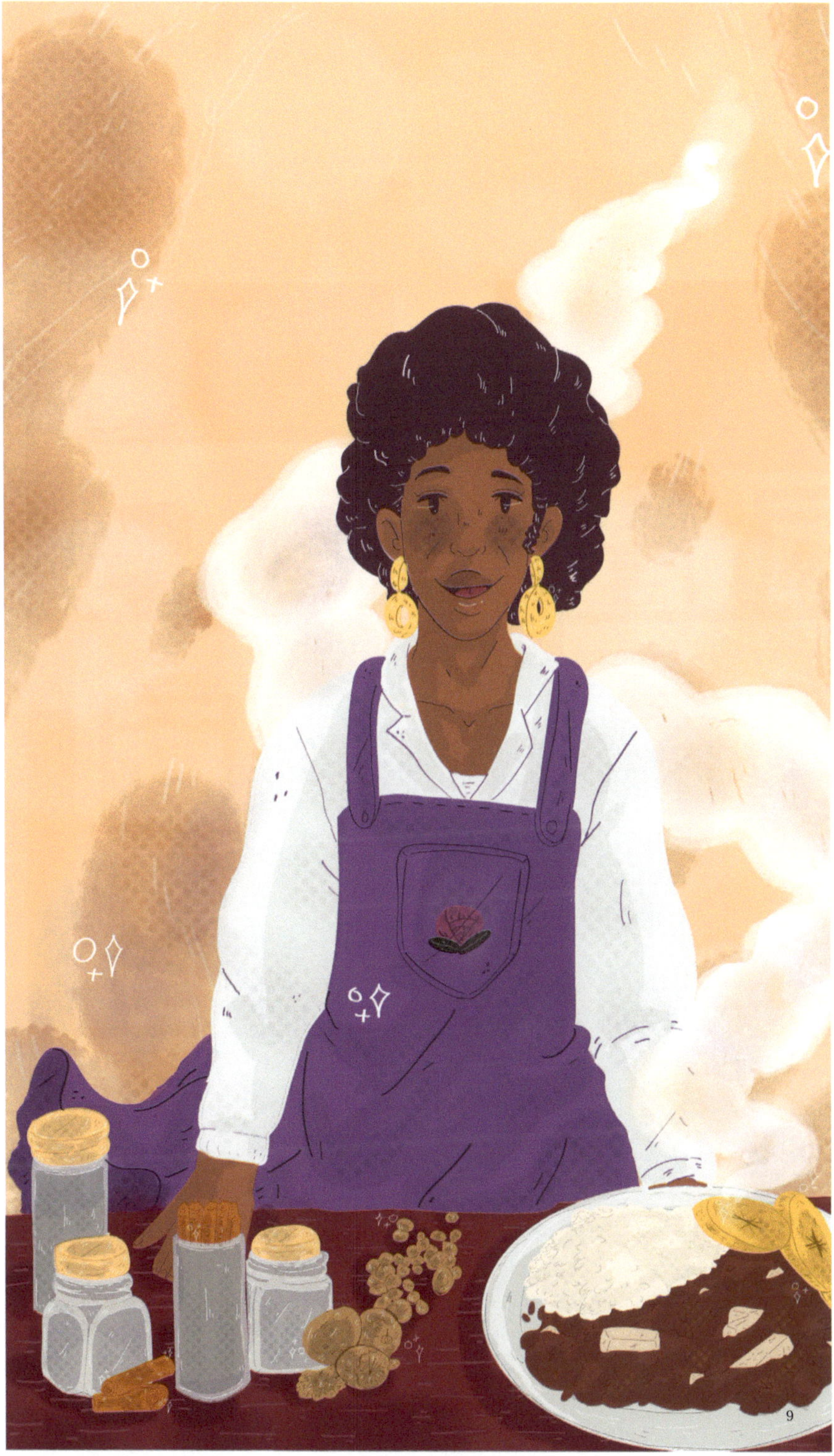

Love & Lust

Cold Shoulder

I have someone
At least I think I do
Keep being pushed away
and I keep on loving you

You're mine
Or at least I thought you'd be
Claiming you as my possession
but was it meant to be?

Mixed signals
hot and cold
Will you stay?
Or should I go?
Know my worth now
and I thought you knew it too

The good outweighs the worst
I just wish it didn't hurt
Battle wounds are deep
although they're few

I'm Fine

You were my exception
to my rule for second chances
I actually forgot about it
blinded by romance and
Now I feel my whole heart
bursting into flames
My heart and mind confused
how I got caught up once again

Being honest and open
only made me vulnerable
Didn't get your way
so your old habits had to show
I have no more excuses
for the way you've treated me

My knight in shining armour?
Oh no you couldn't be

As I'm torn
he sits beside me occupied
Even if he asks
"I'm fine" is my sole reply
Letting him know how I feel
isn't even worth my breath
He'd only realize my worth
if I up and left

Hibiscus

One more chance

For some reason
I just can't learn from this lesson
I've failed this test more than once before
Seen u transform
from ally to foreign in seconds
Forgiveness
is the reason for my low score
Theoretically
I know what I have to do
But application is missing
when it comes to you...

Kishawna

Wishes

All I ever wanted
was a heart that was mine
Was that too much to wish for?

Or should I have used my wish
on something more practical
Like world peace or riches?

Or a way to make sure
my eyelids don't fall off the hinges
From the flood of tears
that relentlessly pour
I've seen others settle
but I needed more
I wanted that connection
that bond
and to be unforgettable
but instead I find myself tryna cope
tryna let it go

my recovery turned out
to be worst than the war
my heart and my mind
now more bruised than before

Replay

Vulnerable, naïve, silly me
Same scene again my new reality
I only blame myself
for what we've come to be
I put too much weight
on the value of you loving me
Idealism was my school of thought
Stayed within range
although you shrugged me off
Only blame myself
for how I feel right now
Knew from the first few times
you love to let me down

Kishawna

Hurt Who?

Baby love.
You have mastered the art
of repressing memories of unpleasantries
Moments that hurt so deep
your heart cannot carry them
You have to let them free.

This is child's play
We've been doing this for decades
Cool as a cucumber letting it all slide

"Why'd you let him hurt you like that?"
"Hurt me?" I respond
Not remembering the instances
of repeated emotional assault
Not remembering
when my voice was held tightly
in my throat
in fear of falling to pieces where I stood

Not a tear will drop here for you
How could they hurt me
when I chose to no longer feel?
When I chose to pretend
till the smiles became real

Hibiscus

New Decor

Added to my Pinterest board
I was counting down the days
Tiptoed around eggshells
Tried to avoid your rage
Chose a palette that reflected me
Rearranged furniture
threw out the sheets
And all remnants of burgundy
A symbol of you loving me
Purple, pinks, and bright yellows
To lift me up when I feel low
Let go of the only love I've known
We grew apart, now I'm alone

Kishawna

Transfer

I passed you every day
Rose-coloured glasses
Unknowingly
sheltering myself from your light
Waded through crowded streets
In search of the main attraction
Longing for someone
to love me back
But you were always there
Just a fixture
in the background
Insignificant
Unmoving
Nine thousand and ten days
I strutted past you
If I was aware of my surroundings
If I would have made use
of all my faculties
I would have known
it was always you
I would have poured
all that love we gave to them
back into us

Chills

Grey sweats look amazing on you
Your eyes wander but never leave me
Unthinkable
Forbidden
Artic
Sun blaze when you choose to

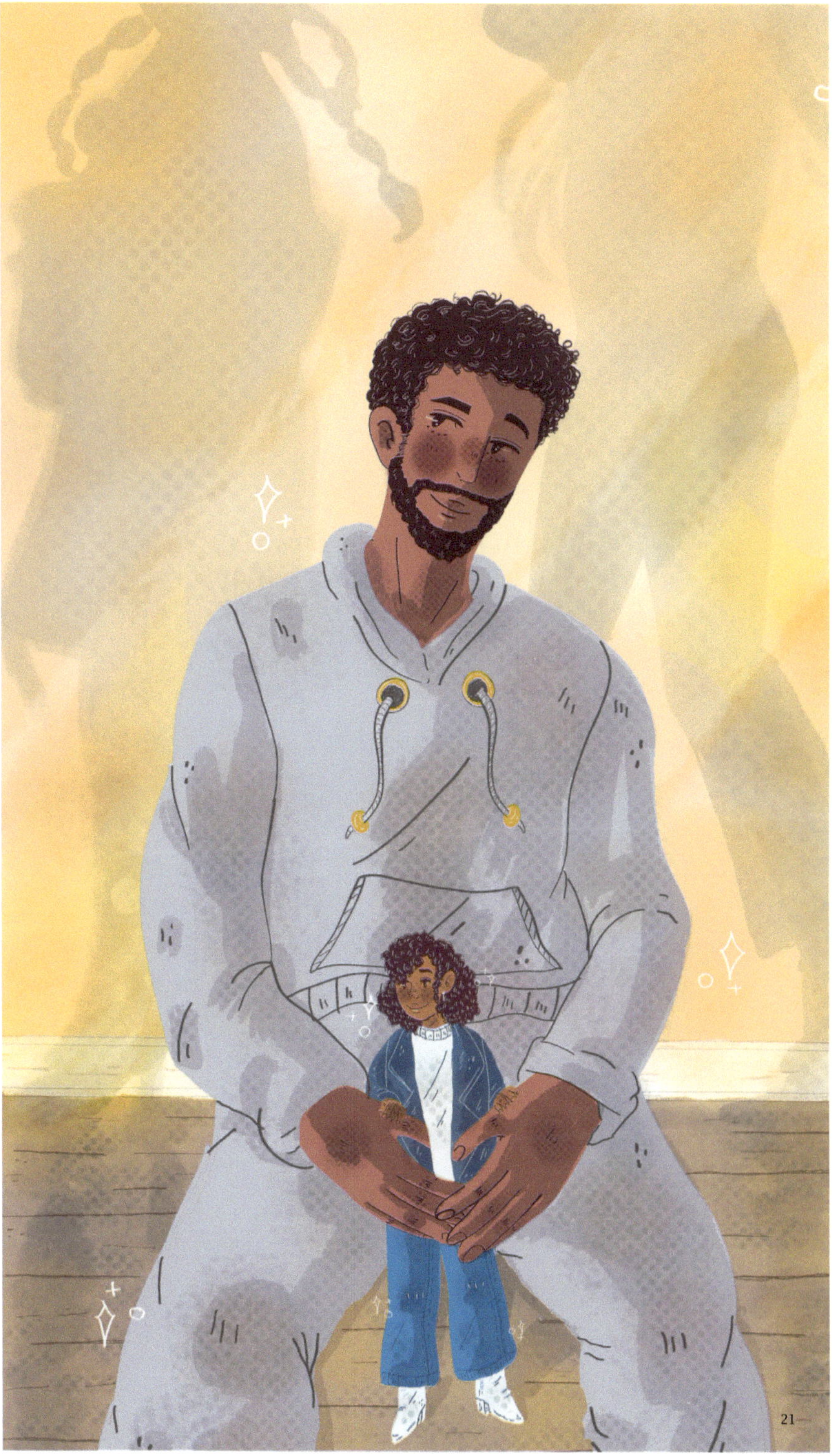

Hibiscus

The fit

I should be okay with less right?
With whatever you decide I deserve?
Despite the fact that I am full
So full
that if the package
contained any more
it would burst?
But I should deny
how much I am for you right?
Try to piece myself
into something you can afford?
Try to fit into the box
you've made custom just for me?
Into shoes that are 3 sizes too small?

Kishawna

Jerk

What were your first thoughts?
When you caught the intensity
of my brown eyes?
Noticed the fullness of my lips
Got a sniff of the coconut oil
on my curls
Did you know then
That your intentions weren't pure
Was it always your goal
to break what you can't have?
Strip the gold from my core?
Rewrite my story
to have no happily ever after

Hibiscus

I'm tired of hiding parts of me
To maintain some false neutrality
You fuel my insecurities
When you don't make time for me

When you don't follow through
Just reminds me what I am to you
A temporary permanent fixture you own
Something that shines
even when she's alone

Something that the maintenance is low
That you don't need to water to grow
Something you can't break
you tried it before
Say that we're friends
but treat me like a whore

I guess you think this is a breeze
You say you'll do better
then put me on freeze
I don't even want more
than what we agreed
You'll probably ignore me after you read

Kishawna

I am hyper-aware of what I have to do
Letting go of you
My love
Is one of the most difficult things
I will have to do.

Hesitation fills my lips
as I notice the words
making their way out.
But feeling small and unimportant
is not my place.

Being vulnerable and disregarded
is not for me.

Questioning my worth
and doubting myself
is the opposite of the woman
I am working so hard to become.

I've convinced myself
that you caring for me is optional.
Lies I tell myself to allow the bar
to sit so low for you
So low
that expectations do not exist.
So low
that you are the exception
to my every rule.
No rules
feel so safe
as to not have any
just live
Low expectations give me the gift
of a sweet nothing or two
a distraction or three
A high unparallel
to any concoction I could create.

I Am

Heart and mind in opposition
When one is present the other's missing
A walking talking contradiction

I am

Fall in love
Facts prove it's fiction
Brain laughing at my new addiction
Move with no logic or restrictions

I am

Eyes front
Heel-toe cause I'm on a mission
I'd know you like me if I only listened
They say I'm blinded by my ambition

I am...

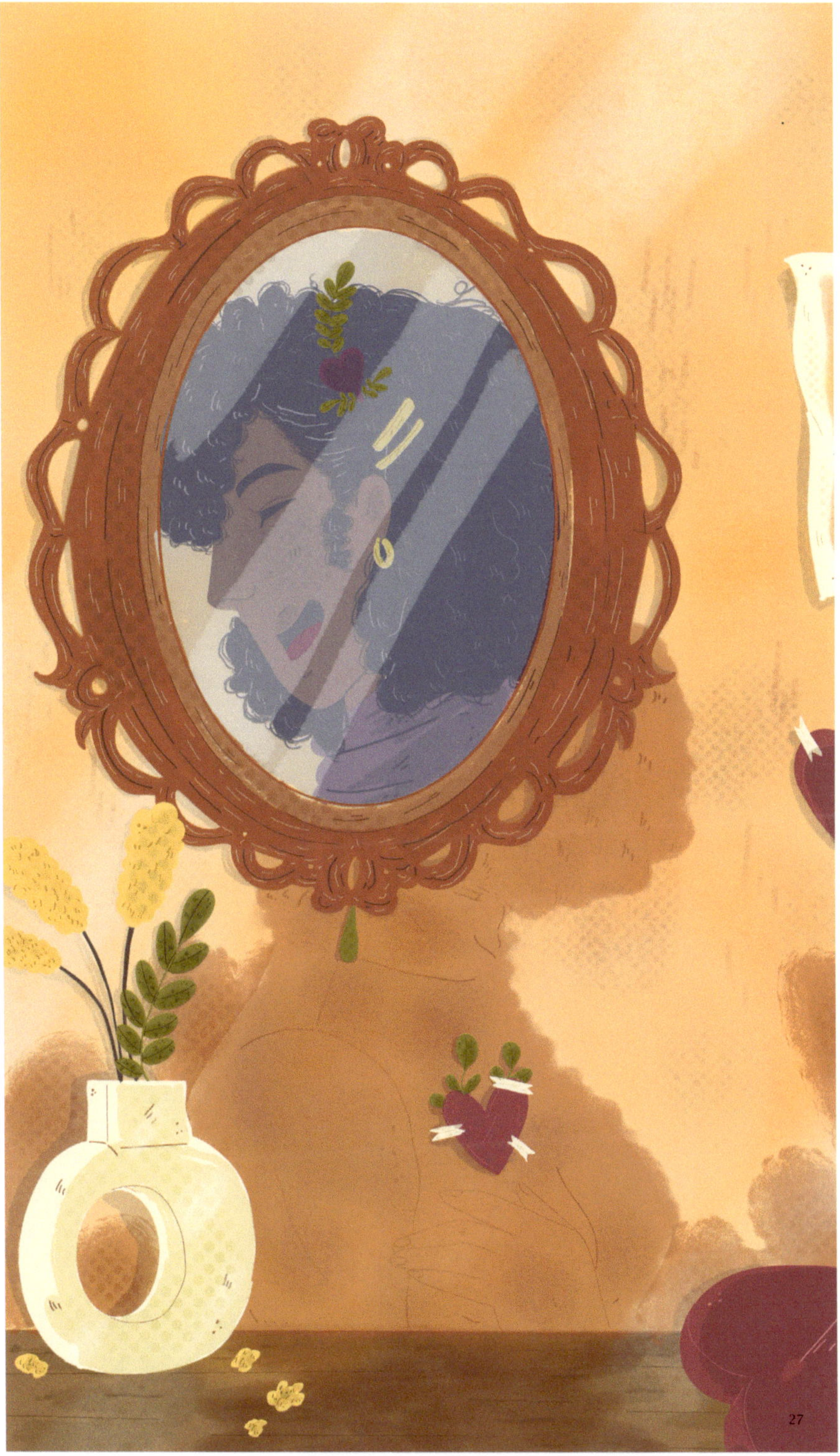

Flame

You say you won't burn me
Old flames
have boasted similar declarations
Fixed their lips
to drip honey out of them for me
Or maybe it was molasses?
The way they slowly
built trust with me
That convinced me
to abandon all defences
Regardless of sugar's manifestation
Each time I'm left scorched
trying to soothe my wounds
I know
I'm not supposed to judge you
by men I've loved before
But if you see the same signs
on a different road
what do you do?

Kishawna

I really wanted you to love me
I wanted you to look at me
and know
that I'm what you've been missing
all along
I wanted you to hear my voice
and wonder
how you ever went without it
I wanted you to feel my touch
and know
every one after mine
would feel like sandpaper

You'd think I'd recognize
that we don't fit
Someone else
should be filling up
the right side of your bed
Someone less ambitious
less argumentative
someone with less fire

A girl that would just feel blessed
that you looked her way
Not someone who sees you as an equal
and recognizes your potential
Not someone who believes
in your dreams
but calls you on your bullshit
You wanted a lighter love
something easy
something simple
But I promise you
every bit of hesitation on your lips
would disappear
if you let yourself experience
a love like mine

Love like mine

No deed

I should call them out by name
All the men whom I belonged to
with no deed
That quietly evade commitment
Because they got all that they need

It's all or nothing with me
They would say the game was fair
I don't require reciprocity
In love
I'm playing solitaire

Kishawna

Weeds

I wish I never met you
I wish you didn't come and ruin my flow
I wish you would've seen me blooming
and let me be
Instead of picking me
Tearing me from my roots
Playing with me
Just to drop me a few blocks away
And pick up a weed.

But I guess that's it though
How could you value everything I am
When you're used to weeds?

Package

If the package were any more full
it would buss

Lean in close
Make sure you hear it
Thank God if you get near it
Weak men tend to fear it
I am
Spilling over with gifts
flowing through me
A treat for all your senses
Enjoy and don't correct it
Let go of your defences
I need my package custom made
I've tried to fit into your spaces
Crushing egos on my way

Kishawna

Ice

You deserve love
Still I
Shake icicles loose in my sheets
Mastered my smile
But my armour is weak
Disrupt my rhythm
Cause you think that I'm sweet
Put more on your plate
Than I know you can eat

Check the scene
If I'm quiet
I'm stush and I'm mean
And if I keep the line open
I'm labelled a feen

Fantasize me
Because my curves have no end
Try to get close
They'll even settle for friends

You won't be the first
To try to minimize
My being into
Lips, ass, and a set of thighs
But if you used your mind, heart
Instead of eyes
You'd realize
My body's just the shell of the prize

Hibiscus

I don't think you know me sir
I take calculated risks
You were
Examined
Measured
Observed
Before I proceeded

Love to me is one of the greatest risks
Constantly watered with luxe conversations
dreams of happiness
acts of chivalry
I bloom

To bloom out of my bud
and expose my petals to the elements
I need to be sure
Sure
that you won't blow me over with your ego
or starve me of air
Sure
that I'll feel your warmth
and our troubles never drown me
But wow...

I seem to never be able to outsmart love
He always comes dressed differently
finds a way to creep in
and disguises himself as ideal
And I open
and I fall
I try to retreat back to my bud
Instead
I feel each petal leaving me
slowly
Leaving me
bare
I can't undo opening up
I fall apart instead

35

Hibiscus

Question?

Universe,
Is he the one or just a lesson?
You're running out of curriculum for me
I know I joke about rotations
Belt out creep by TLC
but hear me out
I'll let that go
He feels right
Standing beside me
There are no words
But strong connection
I can feel his energy

Kishawna

Beneath

It may only be a second
I crave connection
You're fine as hell but
Let me see your soul
You trying to hide it
With that handsome smile
is getting rather old
Let me inside
I wanna know
all the secrets you never told
I can tell you know it's safe
Am I coming off too bold?

Karmic

I've loved you before.

Rolling off my tongue
it sounds insane but hear me out
Take time to
listen to our hearts
between the silence
it'll relieve your doubts

I've felt you before
Your energy
Your vibe
Your aura casting wide
you can set aside your pride

Cause we've been here before
Our souls dance in sync
Can't deny this karmic link
Deja vu's the word
I think?

Kishawna

Plot twist

Did you see him too?
Had to ask my girl if you were really real
Thought I just imagined you
Just blinded by what I feel
It's surreal
To be by your side and really feel seen
Pinch myself daytime
Convinced I'm caught up in a dream
Let's fast forward
Tried to escape love
but now you got me cornered
Death by a thousand cuts
No need to call the coroner
I hate games
Showed you my hand
you hid half yours behind your back
Thought we were playing fair
Never thought you'd do me like that

Still reading

Gingerly take you off the shelf
Decoding your history in your spine
Measure your weight
in these hands of mine
What will I find?
If I open you up and turn the pages
Read all about your life phases
How you struggled
heart broke but you still made it
The fact you let me in is so courageous

Let's go

I'm blocked before I even begun
Your text written in foreign tongue
I can't put you down
I learn to read between the lines
Read your pauses as a sign
Translate words that don't exist in mine
Because to me
You're worth the time
Still reading

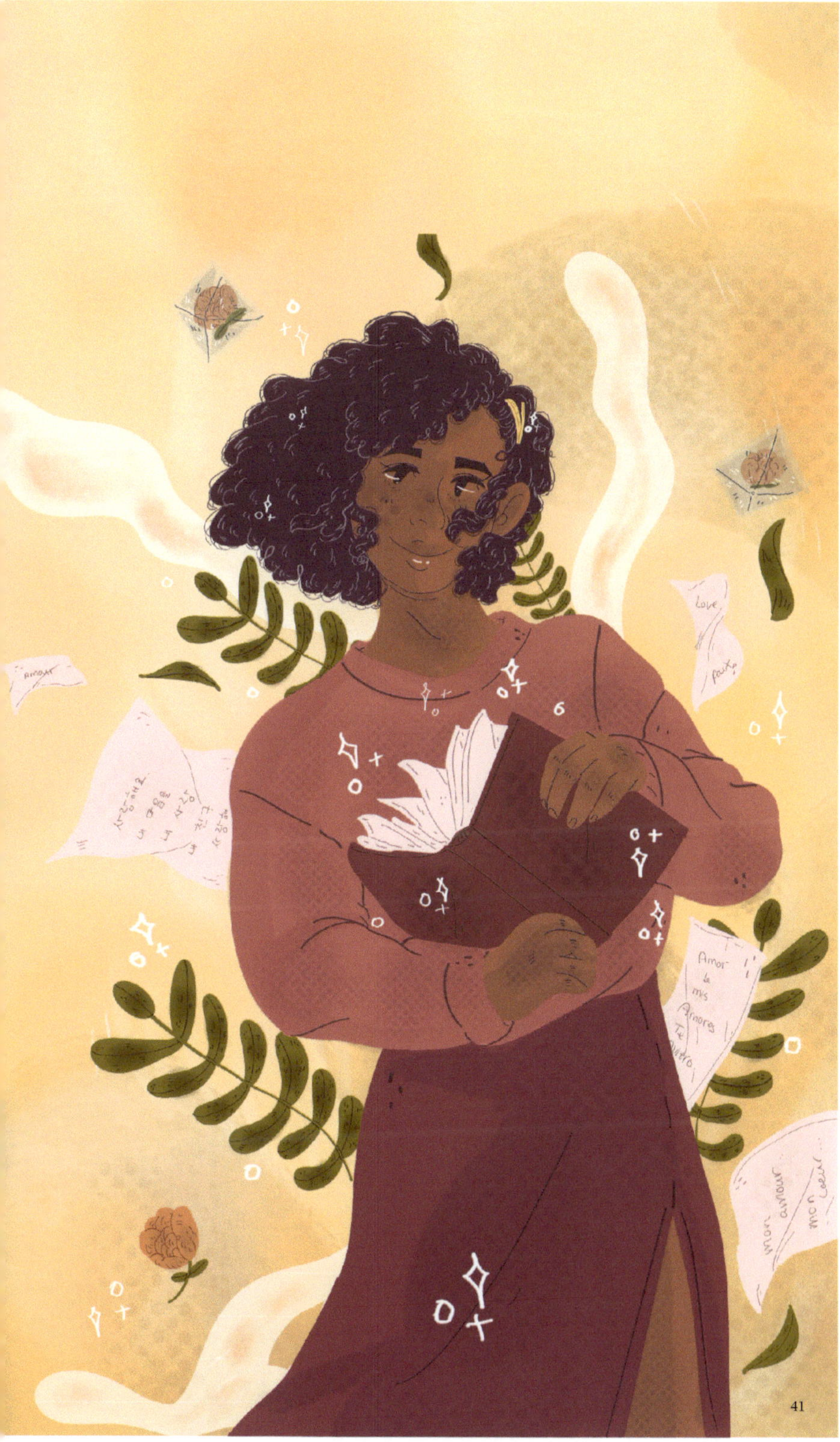
Love
Amor
de
mis
Amores
mon amour

Mental Wellness & Self Care

Again

Every time I allow myself to feel
I'm empty
yet full of regrets
Why do we do this?
Tell me again
what's the benefits
of being true to how I feel?
Tell me again
how leaving my armour at the door
is the right way to love?
I can't
I feel my stomach turn
with the thought
Can you repeat
what's wrong with me again?
Say it loud
so I can hear it echo
on the walls I share
with me myself and I

Kishawna

Therapy

Where's the leak?
They keep escaping
the tightly screwed jar
I banished them to
I don't need these
What use are they?
All they do is weaken me
The imprint on me is thick
Heavy
Although when I try to read it back
Voice tight
eyes full
The ink is barely there
How do I heal
from things I worked so hard to forget?

Hibiscus

Bedtime

I beg my bed please take the weight
Can you just hold these thoughts for me?
If it's not one thing it's another
I swear I won't be long you'll see
I just need a few hours
So I can have a chance to breathe
Don't have anywhere to go
for the comfort that I need

Kishawna

Cover up

They have no idea
They think you're made of stone
Most resilient in the pack?
Can't tell
I feel all alone
They don't see the cracks
How could they?
With this smile
You say you really want to know me
The full version?
Or free trial?

Reach

straight
stretched
strained
Reaching for normal
but routine feels obscene
Eat & sleep? Feels too deep
My goals? They've gone cold
Can I impact the next chapter
that gets told?

What's my role on this stage?
It's okay to be afraid
Triggered by scrolls on IG?
That's just my anxiety
She lives here
not so silently
Trying to express feelings
I denied to me
staying quiet
still.
so I can hear
My purpose shout over my fear

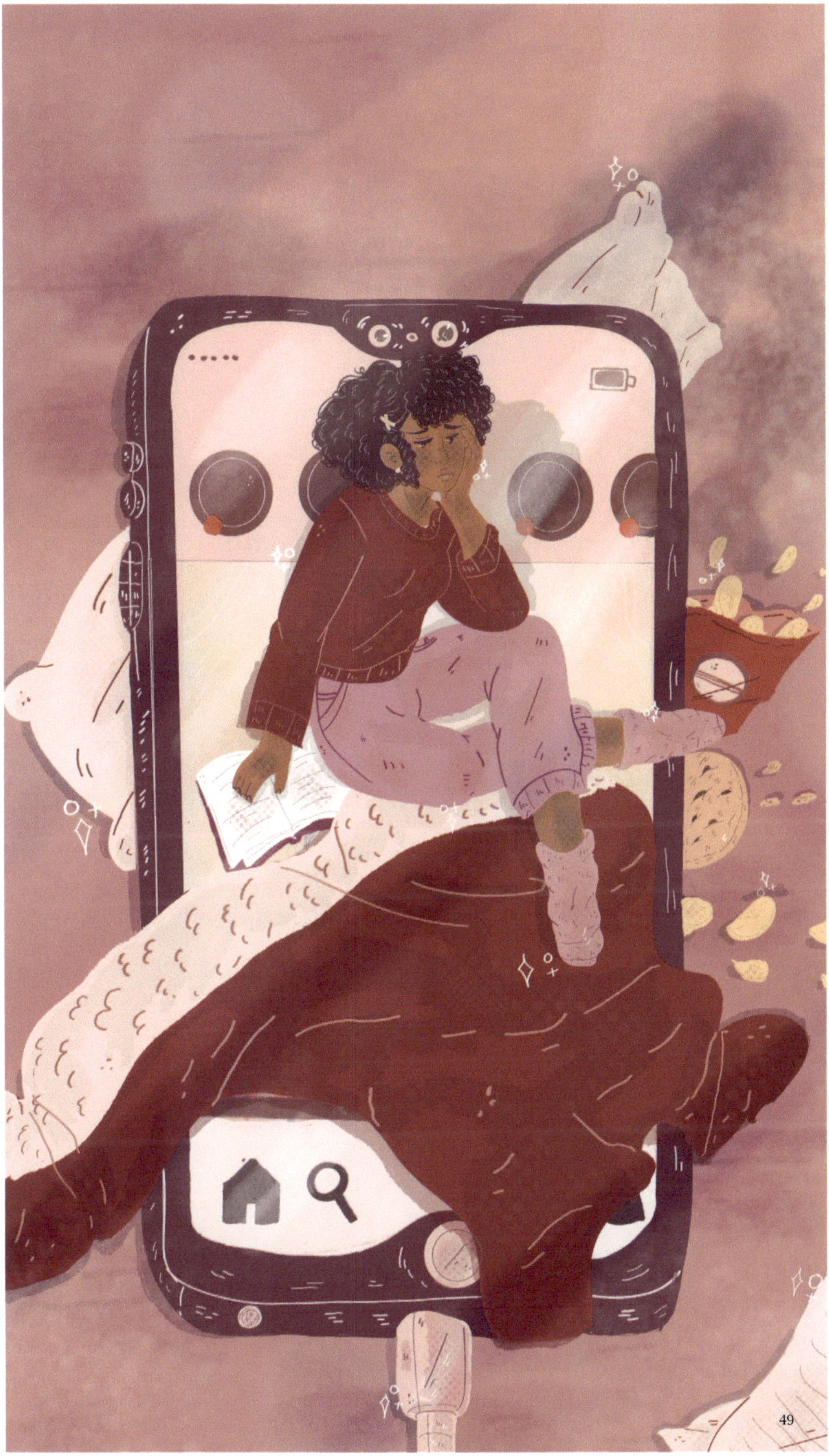

Burnout

Crumbling with every exhale
I know I need a break
Eyes wide
But check the detail
Overdrive's my constant state
You'd think I'd learn from times before
Fruits of my labour
reap rotten fruit at the core
Basics
Elementary
Like how many seashells
did Sally sell by the seashore
All games aside
I hear my body screaming loud
"When last did we
just sit and watch the clouds?"
"When last did we
do it for us and not the crowd?"
"When last did you
check-in with your inner child?"
"We know you say you got it
but that girl is running wild"

Kishawna

Anxiety

Shaking the feeling off my bones
Yet it seems it's reached my marrow
Fighting eyelids
To escape night terrors
Awake me or asleep me who's fairer?
No response to that question after hellos

And I've tried to slow these thoughts
Burn sage and meditate to start my day
Breathe in and out just like you say

But I'm telling you something's off
I feel a shift deep in my core
I can't dismiss it anymore
Can't Band-Aid it like before

I need to look
And force myself to see
The braver, vulnerable side of me
The side begging to be free

But what's free?

Watering

Washing the day away
Gently watering the flower that is me
Taking time to hear my needs
In here
No one else to please
Lathering every crease
From my crown down to my feet
Pondering what life really means
Opening from all the steam
Close my eyes and just pretend
I'm on a beach with golden sand
Ignore the pruning of my hands
Dream long enough to get a tan
These moments are critical
My half breaths turn back to full
I end my session exactly when
My roots are nice and damp again
A time when I can selfishly
Pour extra love inside of me

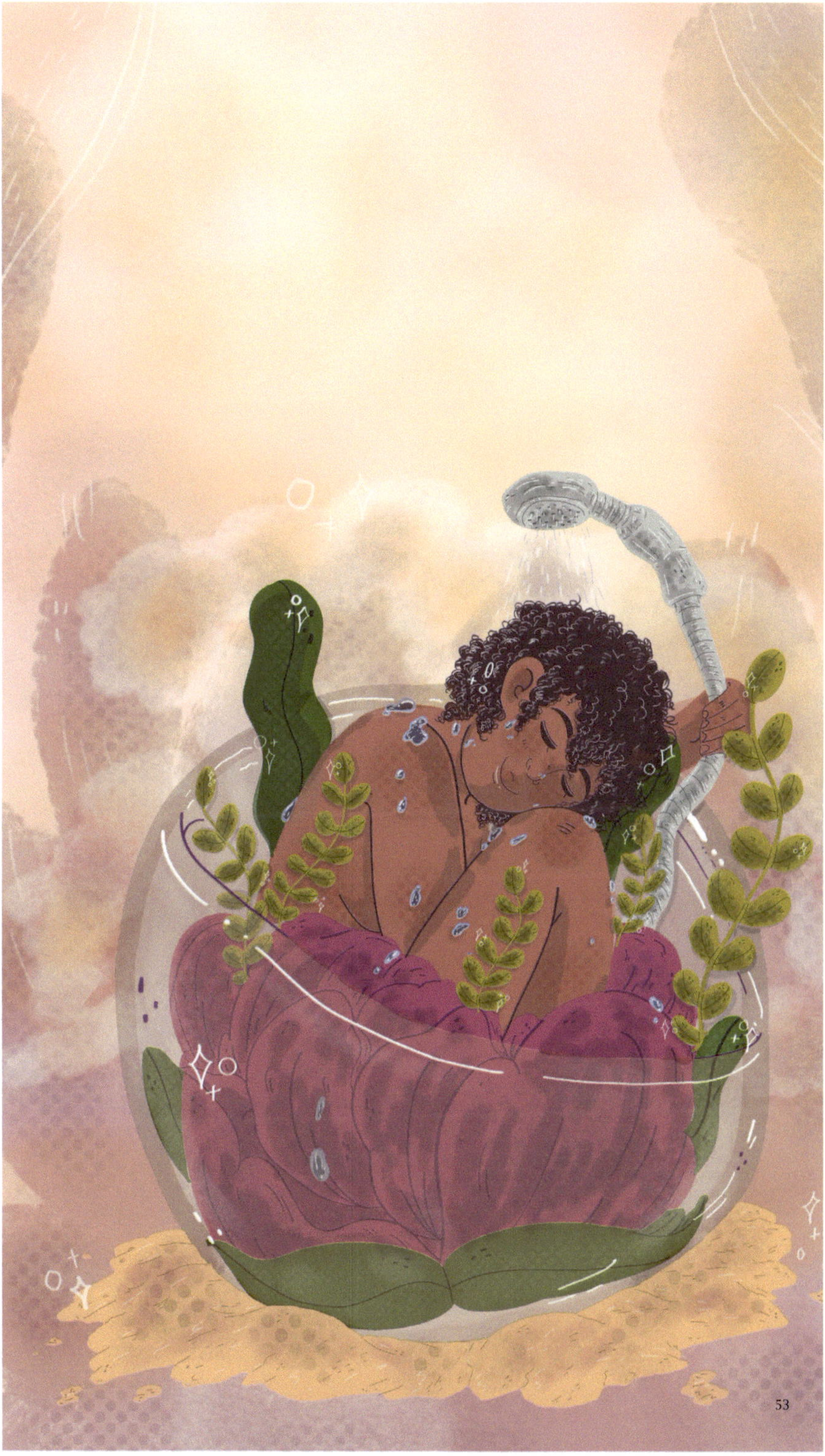

Hibiscus

Saturday

Slowly peeled them open
I feel cheated I can't lie
6:05 Saturday morning
My body's screaming why

The silence and the knowing
That the day belongs to me
Natural rise no alarm going
Notice opportunity

Outside your 9 to 5
what will you do with this blank slate?
It's all on you to decide
Will you rest or will you create?

Kishawna

Home

I have yet to find the place
Where I fit in
where I belong
Where the language I speak
is the mother tongue

You wouldn't know
how it is to have no home
To be in rooms full of familiars
but know that you're alone
To consider disappearing
From this body that you own

Can't put my armour down
Always ready for the war
Can't sleep at night
They're breaking down my door
Can't recall the last time
I truly felt secure
I need to find home
can't live out of boxes anymore

Compassion

Imagine my surprise
When you met my pain
with a gentle touch
I wish I was that kind
when I felt it rising within me
Rushing quickly
From the soles of my feet
Until shamelessly
flirting with the rim of my eyes
For years I pushed it down
A glossy glare
was the most it got from me
Tipping a toe in deep conversation
A nervous laugh or three
We don't have time
Just close the box
Instead
I decided to just take a peek
But I couldn't look away
did you always love me?
I asked
dreading the answer
You replied
I never missed a day

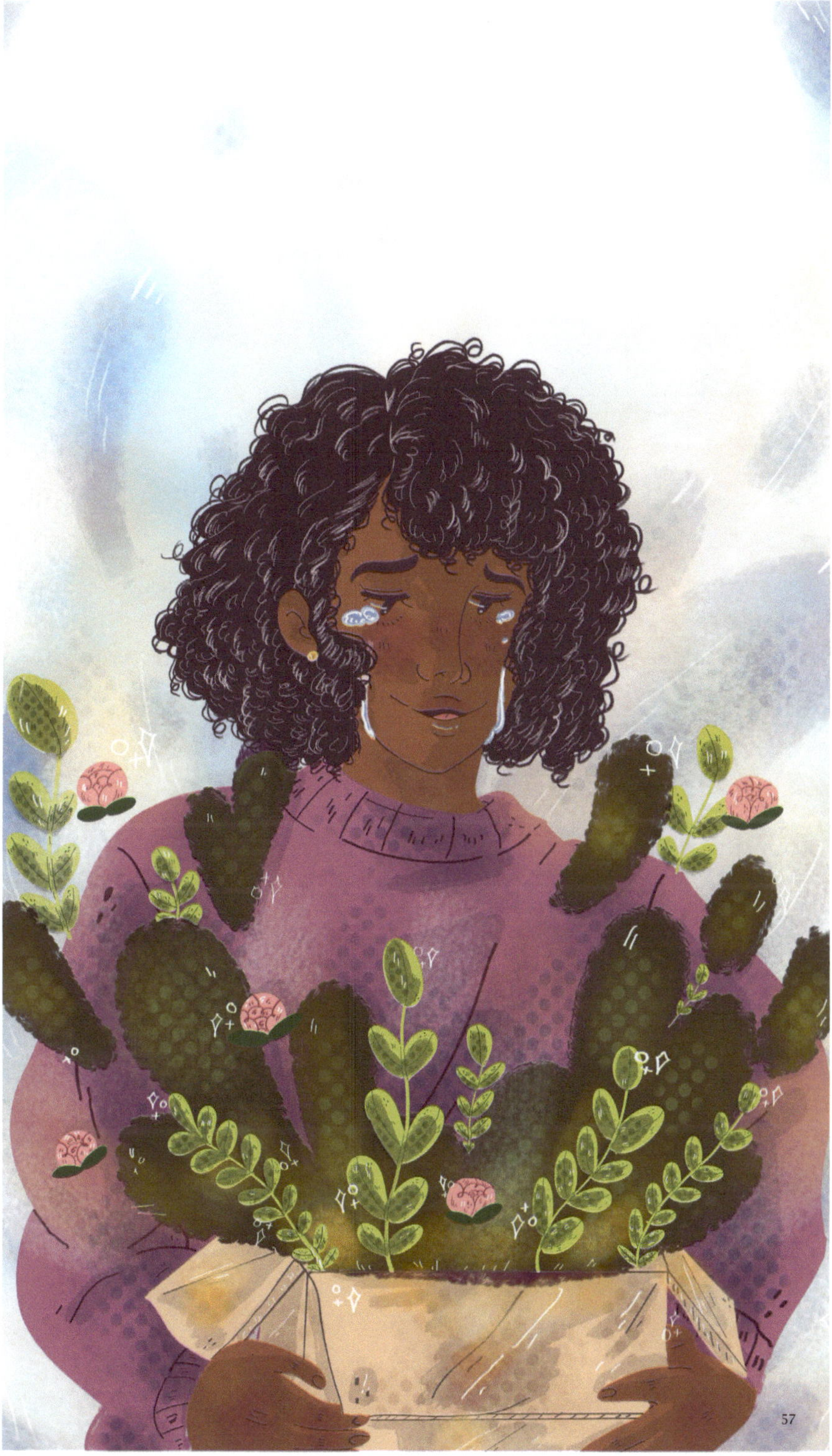

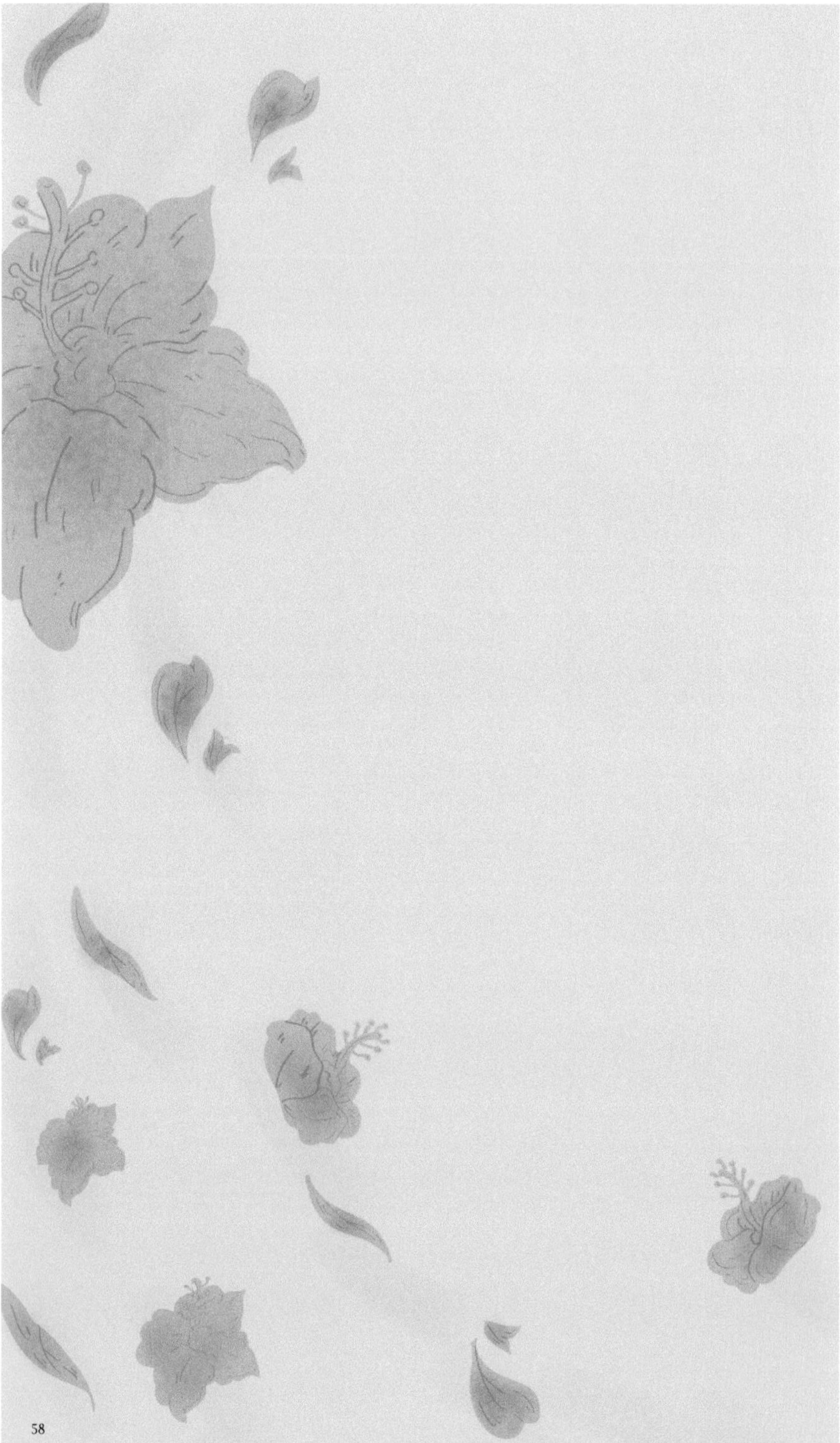

Work & Career

Hibiscus

My problem is...

My problem is...
My potential is boundless
but I'm limited by time
I'm colouring my life
deliberately outside the lines
I can't fit in your box
of what you think I should be
Despite what you say
I'll always be me
I've push myself further
than I thought I could
I'm accomplishing things
they never thought I would
I prove to myself
every day I'm brilliant
I rise above it
proving my resilience
Multidimensional
Driven
and dreaming
Executing these plans
I've been scheming
My problem is...
I have no problem at all
I just won't be contained
to avoid your feeling small

Kishawna

Webs

Light as air
Still will wrap you in
Delicate, intricate
Don't know where it ends
or it begins
While you sleep, I weave my traps
I rest when daylight comes
No need to hustle for my food
The hard work's already done
By the time you realize
It's already way too late
Did you really think I would leave
my survival up to fate?
I eat my fill
Lay back and chill
Enjoyed a meal well earned
Could leave fragments of you here
A lesson your kind won't learn

Hibiscus

Pronounciation

Which blade have you chosen today?
To butcher my name
I know your favourite blade's serrated
Have you ever thought to take note
of how my letters are thoughtfully
arranged?
Feel the rare melodic weight
Dance across your tongue
Before denying me
The only thing I truly own

Kishawna

Initiation

Through gritted teeth
I
Sipped on the poison
Half convinced I was immune
Placing the weight
On my resilience
to bring me back to health
I knew I was swimming
through toxic waters
Littered with smiling faces
I mistook for a warm welcome

Champions

Thank you for seeing me
I'm exhausted trying to navigate
Through these halls
With these people
Causing my self-doubt to inflate
I'm not in the rooms
But I know you fight for me
You discreetly lick your wounds
And march again
Decisively

Kishawna

Resilience

I can tell you're trying to break me
And I mean
Once upon a time
I would've cared enough to fight back
But I'm tired of going rounds with you
Take your best shot
Let the pieces fall as they may
Do you not know
who you're fucking with?
I will build empires out of my shards

White feminism

What a luxury
To have mountains fall to their knees
When the faint scent of you
catches breeze
How do you not trip on the debris?
In your stilettos head high
Crushing necks beneath your platforms
Deaf to the cries
You do what you want how you want
No need to compromise
When I was younger
I used to want to be just like you
Lost myself in the dark
Exhausted trying to pay my dues
We're not the same you and I
I'm too many deviations apart
I can't operate like you
Cause I got too much heart
I can't operate like you
You're way too bold
My skin colour hue
Used to be branded and sold
I won't operate like you
You're way too cold
If you had my hand
I'm sure you'd fold

67

Black in Tech

Guess I took you by surprise
you weren't expecting me here
Firm, rooted, capable
was it my melanin?
or the kink in my hair?
was it my feminine?
I'd love if you could share
your attempts to reduce me
are null and void here

Black Woman In Tech
barely shown you a preview
work ethic bar none
excellence is my prelude
used to worry
my perspective's been renewed
Tuck it in
your privilege
is starting to protrude

Kishawna

Unlearning

We walk side by side
But my stride is different than yours
Confidently I glide
but you don't see the tip and the toe
You knock
I hesitate to even open the door
Are you sure your intentions are pure?

Can't tell who has my back anymore
I'm the ROI my ancestors fought for
It seems we won some battles
but now they're starting the war

Unlearning

I rise
cold sweats
doom thick in the air
Our very existence being questioned
They're letting lions out of the lair

You don't see the anxiety
your neutral creates
How it's all on the line
discussing how I'm feeling of late
How I breathe knowing
that I'm taking up space
Risking what I worked for
being taken off of my plate

Kishawna

Unlearning

Went through your system
successfully assimilate
I navigate your society
that is rooted in hate
I learned your history
I even let you narrate
How you discovered occupied lands
and built countries so great
Now that I'm older
It's plain to see
You hid the violence and theft
so eloquently
You made me question my value
to the utmost degree
Black bodies no shackles
but never mentally free

Existential

How can you deny me of my form?
Of who I am
Of all I've been
Since the moment I was born?
Why is your main objective
To dim my light
Mute my perspective?
These used to torture my directive
Till I got honest and reflective
When you get to hold the sun
When the wars of men are done
When the sun rises in the west
When dead men rise up to confess
That's when I'll surrender
My self-worth to my offenders
My talents and my light
To those without foresight
Put my dreams high up on a shelf
When you lack mastery of self
Sacrifice my divinity
When you lack humility
Give up what to me is elemental
When your problem's existential

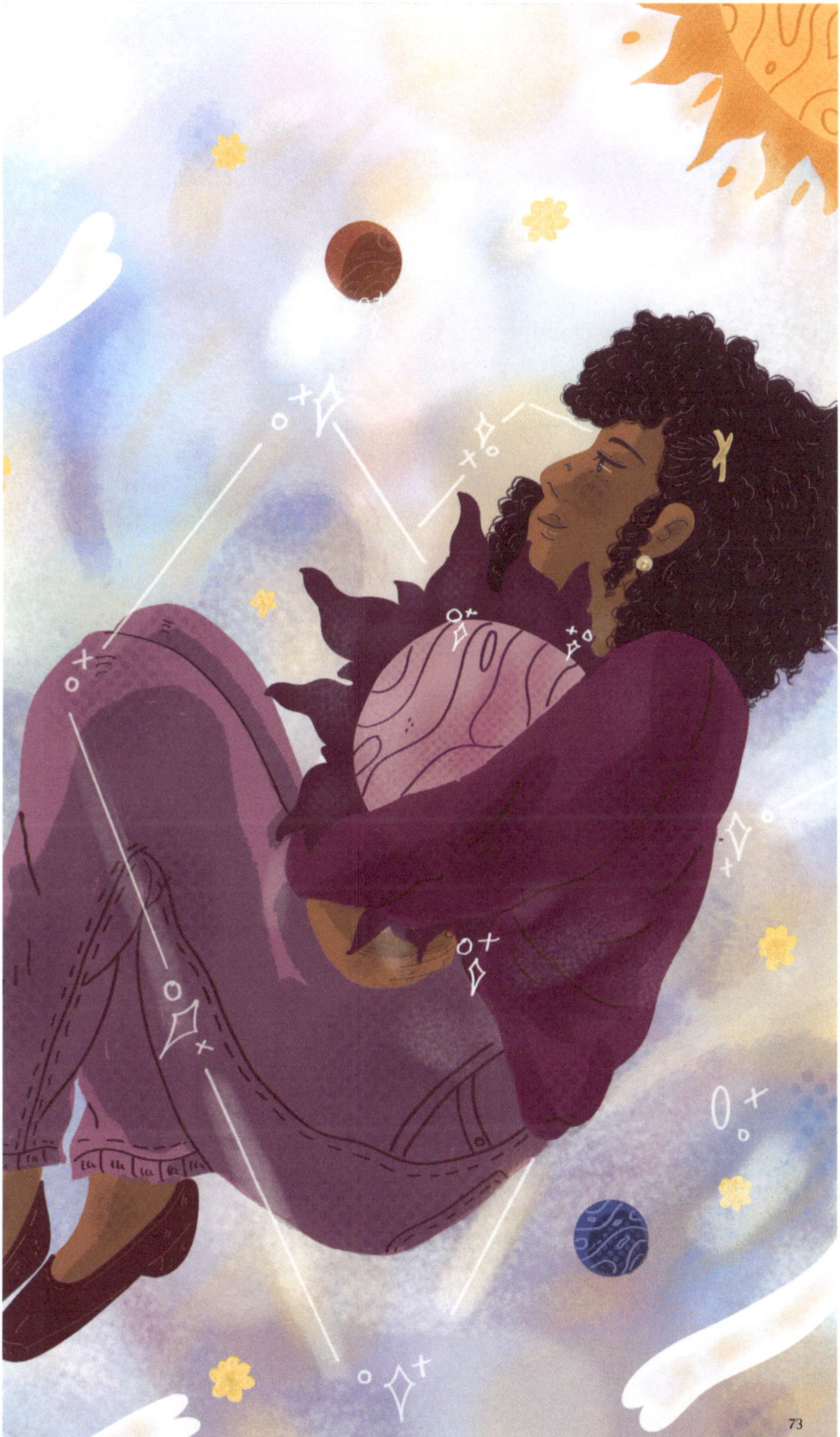

Acknowledgements

Thank you for reading this book in its entirety! I hope these poems granted you a peek into my world. If you see yourself in any of them that's truly the greatest gift for me. This is a labour of love and I'm so grateful to everyone who has believed in me and helped me along the way. It was immense self-reflection and finding myself again that led me back to poetry. I love to sing and my poems when I was younger were the product of songs I wrote that I forgot the tune to.

I'd first like to thank my parents. They've nurtured my artistry throughout the years. My mom would practice with me for talent shows, and my dad and I would set up the tape recorder in the living room and experiment with different riddims. Despite not seeing my talent as a career path, they unequivocally supported me. I remember when I was in elementary school, they saw me selling my poems for $1 and to my utter surprise, they let me to continue.

Grandma, Auntie Paula, and Auntie Vivette I know you're all always with me. I felt each of you guiding my steps through this.

My sisters and friends, can you believe this? A real book in your hands with my name on it? It would not have been possible without you. Thank you for always giving me feedback in the group chats and cheering me on to the finished line. Special shout out to Shadéa, Simone, Richee, Yurissa, Latty, Roshiana, Arya, Cherise, Jemila, Jovell, Stephanie, Kwanta, Yvonne, Samantha, and Aaliyah. Your feedback and encouragement really set the stage for me to start believing I can do it!

Mélissa Mathieu, you breathed life into my poems through your art. I never could have imagined such vibrant and accurate depictions of my poetry.

Last but not least, I'd like to thank my experiences. I went to my first therapy appointment in June 2019. It took me a year to even set up an appointment. I was so reluctant to go. There is a lot of stigma around mental health in the Black community and the Caribbean community. Therapy helped me process emotions I was repressing. I have this saying that I put things I don't want to feel or talk about in a box on a shelf. Well, the shelf was beginning to break. I had to start taking boxes off the shelf and gently begin exploring what I've gone through. Writing these poems is my way to acknowledge my wounds and my achievements instead of pretending neither exist.

Let me know what you thought of the book by leaving a review on my site or Amazon. You can also send me an email at iamkishawna@gmail.com.

Want to stay in touch?
Sign up for my newsletter at kishawna.com for information on new releases and merchandise.
You can also find me on socials at @iamkishawna.

Hibiscus

Sorrel Recipe

Ingredients:

1 bag of dried sorrel
Peeled and chopped fresh ginger
handful of pimento
J. Wray & Nephew Red Label Wine* (optional)
Wray & Nephew White Overproof Rum* (optional)
Brown sugar to taste
3 litres of boiling water
Metal bowl or pot

Only if of legal drinking age where you are

Kishawna

1. Put dried sorrel, ginger, and pimento in a bowl/pot
2. Cover with boiling water overnight. Put a cover on to hold steam in.
3. The next day, take out the pimento from the bowl.
4. Strain half of the mixture into another bowl or jug.
5. Blend the other half of the mixture. It should have the dried sorrel and ginger in it.
6. Strain the blended mixture.
7. Repeat steps 5&6 until finished.
8. Sweeten to taste
9. Add alcohol to your discretion.

Hibiscus

About the Author

Kishawna is a Canadian creative who infuses her island roots of Jamaica into her art. She is a data professional and diversity in STEM advocate by day. She began writing and singing from a very young age and has rediscovered art as a way to express the process of unbecoming who she never was. She finds inspiration in the small rhythms of life best exemplified in her poems, webs and watering. She is excited to continue exploring her creativity and to share her poetry with a broader audience.

Kishawna

About the Illustrator

Mélissa Mathieu is an illustrator based in Montreal, Canada. At a young age, her love for cartoons and anime brought on a great passion for drawing. Her artistic references and inspiration come from fashion editorials, Japanese animations, gastronomy, personal memories, and cute aesthetics. Her style revolves mostly around watercolors, pastel colors, as well as soft and cute looks and concepts. She mainly works with self-portraits and illustrations of black women but enjoys working on a great variety of subject matters. Melissa has a particular talent for capturing the essence of her characters with great facial expressions and expressive body language.

Lightning Source UK Ltd.
Milton Keynes UK
UKHW051347260221
379415UK00001B/19